Fossils of a fleeting life

Musings on Love, Loss, and Everything
In Between

Aninda Halder

BookLeaf
Publishing

India | USA | UK

Made with ❤ on the BookLeaf Publishing Platform
www.bookleafpub.in
www.bookleafpub.com

For the moments we carry,

For the ones we leave behind,

And for you, dear reader—

May you find yourself in these pages.

Acknowledgement

This book is made of fragments—moments, people, and emotions I couldn't let go of. To my friends: thank you for being my constant, for grounding me when I drifted too far, and for revealing parts of myself I couldn't see.

To the people I've loved: you've left indelible fingerprints on my heart. In some way, every poem here owes its existence to you. Some of these words were written in joy, others in the hollow aftermath of your absence. Either way, you've shaped me more than I can admit.

To my younger self, scribbling words late into the night: thank you for feeling everything so intensely, even when it hurt. You didn't know it then, but you were building something that would outlast those moments.

And to you, the reader: thank you for holding this book and letting my words find a place into your world. Without you, these poems would have remained tucked away, unread and unresolved.

This book is my way of making sense of the fleeting, the painful, and the beautiful. Thank you for helping me hold onto it.

Preface

This book isn't just a collection of poems—it's a personal fossil record, preserving who I've been at different moments, in different skins.

The earliest pieces emerged from a schoolboy's narrow world, where afternoons stretched endlessly, and the future felt as distant as it was boundless. Others reflect a college student's struggle to stand on his own, making sense of love, loss, and that unsettling feeling of not quite fitting into the puzzle.

Some were scribbled late at night by an IIMB graduate who wanted to believe he finally understood where he was headed, yet couldn't shake the quiet doubts pressed in around him.

And now, there are lines from someone shaped by the pressures of brand deadlines, career goals, and an adult's responsibilities—someone who still finds peace in unexpected quiet moments, pen in hand, searching for words that feel like home.

I've chosen not to rewrite these poems, though I'm tempted to. They belong to those earlier versions of myself, with all their imperfections . They speak in voices I no longer quite recognize, reflecting perspectives I've outgrown or come to question. In their rough edges and uneven rhythms, they reveal truths that a polished revision might erase.

As you read, I hope you'll encounter not just my journey but glimpses of your own—old yearnings, faded hurts, small triumphs, and the stubborn hope that keeps us moving forward, even when we're unsure of the destination.

Thank you for opening these pages. Thank you for letting these moments—confused, hopeful, uncertain —find their way into your life. In some small way, I hope they remind you that none of us move through time without leaving fragments behind.

CONTENTS

Section 1: Love

"Every heart sings a song, incomplete, until another heart whispers back."

—Plato

Love is a fleeting spark, a tempest, a quiet sigh—each moment shaping us in ways we never anticipate. These poems offer glimpses of love's tender beginnings and its lingering echoes.

Orange Blossoms

A summer sunshine peeks through the broken
window.
Let me be the shadow that falls over your
eyes,
Guarding you while you sleep, as time softly
flies.
Let me be with you for the first sip of your
summer morning tea,
And watch you blush in orange, as my
summer blossoms free.

Let me hold you close over leaves fallen dry,
And we'll lay there together, staring at the
blue sky.
Let the wind blow, so her hair falls over my
face;
I'll just sniff my nose and quietly listen to
what she says.
Let me take you to that brownie place you
love,
And we'll share an ice cream, even if we don't
starve.
Let me hold your hand as we walk down the
lane,
And I'll carry the umbrella, even without the
rain.
Let me speak my heart out—just listen to
what I want to say:
I love you brighter than the brightest of every
summer's ray.

***

*The warmth of the first glance lingers, but love finds its
depth in shared silences.*

***

Strangers in the Night

A coffee at a bookstore—sounds like the perfect
date.
So that's where I invited her, the first time we
met.
We agreed on Bahrisons, Galleria Market.
"Hey, I'll be there by eight—have you left yet?"

She wore a green sweater over a sharp black
suit.
I wondered: Did she even change after work?
Her smile was warm, her gaze disarming—
A quiet intensity that felt steady yet charming.

We browsed the shelves, sharing our favourite
reads.
I suggested *The Unbearable Lightness of Being.*
Over coffee, we lingered, lost in conversation.
"How about a drive and some dinner?" I asked.

We caught a cab to my place, to pick up the
car—
In that quiet moment, I first held her hand.
I passed her an AirPod—"What's your favourite
band?"
She played Sinatra's "Strangers in the Night"—
For a romantic cab ride that choice felt just
right.

I drove her into Delhi, to The Piano Man—
A jazz club, my impress-her plan.
But finding seats there was quite a task,
So I held her wrist, leaned in, and asked,
"Think we'll find a spot in that corner, at last?"

She coughed softly, and I called the waiter,
"Can we get some warm water, please?"
Later, she told me it was that small gesture
That made her heart flutter and put her at ease.

She wrapped her arm around mine,
Her head resting softly on my shoulder.
We stood, dazed by the music—
John Mayer's "I Don't Trust Myself (With
Loving You)"—
And I wondered if I could ever trust myself
enough.
Little did I know what this place would mean;
A year later, in this very spot,
I'd sit by her side, knowing—
That she is the one
I'll spend my forever with.

A Summer Noon

I was late to our first date.
Zomato and Google Maps ditched me.
The summer sun scorched me—
So yes, I was late to our first date.

Sweaty and breathless, I walked in the room.
She sat there waiting, lost in her phone's
bloom.
I smiled as I saw her, then our eyes met.
At least I made it; our table was set.
"Hey, I'm sorry. I didn't mean to be late."

She frowned, but her eyes smiled—well, that's
enough said.
We talked and we laughed over paneer tikka
kababs.
She spoke of her life, her joys, and her drabs.
Her spirit was free, and I got lost in the
moment's spree.

Then we walked together beneath summer's
clouds,
Through bustling streets and chaotic crowds.
She was a chatterbox—funny, intellectual.
The time felt rare, delightfully unintentional.

And finally our paths diverted at a signal
place.
She wasn't mine to be with. Her heart
belonged to someone else.

The Longest First Date

Hey, let's catch up at a cafe tomorrow sometime.
Would love to know your life and talk about mine.
Does Indiranagar work? Cafe Max at four?
"Cool, I'll be there—it's a date for sure."

What should I wear now? Maybe a shirt that's white,
A spritz of mild perfume to go with—it feels right.

"I'll be there in about twenty. What about you?"
"Cool, see you there. I've booked a table for two."

Hey K, so what brings you to Bangalore?
Conversations with her were definitely not a bore.
Sunlight kissed her as it peeked through the window;
We enjoyed some wine, our words flowing slow.

K felt honest, genuine, and real—
Opening up to her wasn't a tough ordeal.
"Let's grab some chai?"
I kept buying time with her, and I knew why.

She decided to take me to a grocery market.
I held her hand as she picked stuff for her basket.
She mentioned she makes a mean pasta dish.
"Shall we cook at my place?" I voiced my wish.

We drove back, listening to an old love song.
She held my hand and stole a kiss that was
long.
K decided to spend the night over.
Time felt so good with her, even sober.

She slipped into my t-shirt, her bare toes
tiptoeing in the kitchen.
Watching her cook with grace, I stood
charmed and smitten.
The pasta smelled amazing, and I was in
love—with the food.
I poured the chardonnay, and the air felt
good.

K and I talked about our night and what it all
meant.
She felt more real than someone I could have
dreamt.

Almost 29 hours later, our date neared its
end.
K mentioned, "Hey, at seven, I need to go see
a friend."

She wore a pink top and blue denims as she
booked her cab,
And as she was leaving, life already started to
feel drab.

"K, are we keeping in touch?"
"We'll be in different cities—I can't promise
much."

Little did I know she'd move in with me a few
months later,
And we'd build a love story I'd hold close
forever.

She'd bake cakes that filled the air with
warmth,
Leave little notes tucked in corners, her way
of showing care.

She'd write me letters before my flights,
thoughtful and kind,
And kiss me goodnight with a tenderness that
stilled time.

Those quiet gestures, those everyday joys,
Made it feel like I'd found someone amidst
life's noise.

I walked her to her cab and kissed her
goodbye.
Had no idea this romance would one day die.
Little did I know what was gonna happen
next—
And that was the story of how I met my ex.

***

A city never forgets its people; its whispers live on in
the hearts they leave behind

***

Where the Heart Pauses

I pen a plot for the city that nurtured me,
Kolkata—I left you for a world to see.
I was eighteen when I moved away,
To conquer dreams and pave my way.

Unsure of the joy I was hoping to find,
Let me tell you about what I left behind:

The sound of Rabindra Sangeet from a
crackling radio;
blue buses halting at every patio.
The yellow haze of Ambassadors rushing by,
Street food scents spiral, painting the sky..

This City of Joy, a heartbeat, an emotion,
A city slowed amidst the clock's fleeting
motion.
We pause in our ways— we call it "lyaadh,"
Is there wisdom in chasing every passing fad?
Adda thrives with our kulhad-served teas,
Afternoon naps stolen as time flees.

Red-brick buildings defy the years,
Flurys breakfasts—a ritual that endears.
Culture and heritage linger in the air,
Sunsets at Princep Ghat—a sight to stare

A city where artists and poets find their
place,
Durga Puja fills every heart with grace.
Puchkas spice up every street-side delight,
And biryani with aloo just feels right.

Kolkata, though time stretches us apart,
You remain the keeper of my heart.
I chased the world, yet nothing could replace,
The joy of your warmth, my forever embrace.

A Valentine Note

Maybe I'll find you, concealed behind your
wings, my angel.
I can't forbear the thought of you; I long for a
love story to tell.
I sit down dreaming, wondering what you'd be
like.
Maybe you're a reflection of every girl I've loved
in my life.

Beautiful—the only word I'll remember when I
look into your eyes,
And maybe I'll drown in them, as they drizzle
apart from lonely skies.
The sweetest voice to sing me a lullaby each
night.
A number to text good morning at the sun's
first sight.
A kiss on my nose before I drift off to sleep.
A hand to wipe away the tears I might weep.

The girl who inspires me to write her a song
every day.
The sweetest soul for whom my guitar would
play.
Someone who pushes me to be the best I can be.
A love that keeps me smiling when the world's
against me.

I really want you to hold me tight—
But don't bite my ears while we're out for a
ride!
I'd steal your chocolate ice cream, just for fun,
And you'd chase me through dreams until the
day is done.

Even being apart, your thoughts wouldn't leave
me alone.
You can call me at work, cooking for me over
the phone.
I'd hold your hand as your head rests on my
shoulder at the movies,
Then pillow-fight in the car and kiss after a
chocolate smoothie.

I'd watch you blush in my white shirt, hiding
behind the curtain.
You're still not here, and maybe that's my only
burden.
I'd walk with you at daybreak and drive beyond
twilight,
Holding you till dawn beneath the blanket that
veils the night.

I sit, I sleep, I talk, I breathe—you're in my
every heartbeat.
I eat, I read—it's you I need; my lips just long
for yours to meet.
I promise to cherish and replay every memory
of you in my head.
Just don't leave me, for without you, those
moments would leave me dead.

I'd watch you laugh as your tongue softly touches your lips.
Every lyric, every poem, every tune pleads for you to be mine.
I'd dance a ballet for you amidst the rain,
And keep dancing, even if you call me insane.

I want to be with you through summers and winters.
Say you love me, and I'll protect you from all splinters.
I've written quite a lot, but not all should be planned or told.
At least after reading, you'll know how I wish our story to unfold.

***

Every smile tells a story, and every story leaves its mark.

***

A Portrait of Her Smile

I barely remember our conversations,
The ones we shared during our time.
All I know is a feeling that's familiar—
Every time I reminisce about her smile.

A feeling that soothes my deepest worries,
A smile that lifted me when life got dreary.
Perturbed by memories now blurred,
I scrounge for her smile amidst all the scars.

Recalling how she felt after walking so far,
I sketch a silent portrait from the fragments
left—
One of a smile I remember,
Reliving how it felt.

The Winter Letter

Shivering in the night, I shiver in cold,
Clenching my sheets, seeking the bolster
close.
There are no dreams as the hours unfold—
Just velvet desires, wrapped around a rose.

The rustle of dried leaves, the gusts of wind;
Still is the night, numb to its brink.
My teeth chatter, and thoughts rescind,
Thinking of her, letting my feelings sink.
Guarding my rose from frost and snow,

I penned my words—the ones untold.
I wrote her a letter, a future to sow,
Sealing it with a rose, daring to be bold.

I posted it that night, a night so cold,
Then slept, waiting for her answer,
As my love grew old.

Pages

The pages we turned together at night,
Your numerous questions, your curious sights.
Your childish laugh, your pleasant smile—
I wish to keep hearing it as we walk every
mile.

I notice when you play with your hair, as I
hide from your eyes.
I might even daze, imagining how amazing we
could be, gazing at the skies.
Evasive, I am, of what I feel for you,
Penning words down, emotions that are true.

I lock our memories away for safekeeping,
Hoping you won't break my heart, leaving me
weeping.
Because it's someone else you're already
seeing.

Section 2:
Loss

"What is grief, if not love persevering?"

—WandaVision

Loss is the weight of what slips away, leaving us changed but still searching. These verses linger in absence, finding fragments of meaning in the hollow spaces.

A Tale of Thorns

Let me call her Rose, for I was appalled by her
mesmerising presence.
She was my distant gaze, the end to my torrid
maze.
A blissful calm, a breeze—an enchantment of
pure essence.
Bewitched by her aura, her ways, I dreamt of
her for days.

Let me tell you of the thorns I never knew:
Crescent peaks wrapped in winter's dew.
The unspoken touch has bled me dry,
Yet I don't regret the moments I tried.

Every thorn I touched is a fragment of her memory.
Every drop of blood is etched on some page of our story.

Philophobic

A heartache that fills,
The suffocating torment drills.
I try to run, I try to ignore,
Yet forbidden feelings leave my heart sore.

I try, I try—my demons pry,
Feeding on fears I can't deny.
Hidden insecurities,
Shadows of dread that always creep
My silent ghosts, they linger deep,
Afraid to wake, afraid to sleep.

In my dreams, my emotions rise,
No longer repressed, they catch me by
surprise.

They find me there, raw and true,
Yet I can't choose to love you.

A Mile Away

Even today, when our love's astray,
I watch you from a mile away.
Hearing your voice, I search for my name—
If only things could be the same.

Even today, though we've fallen apart,
I look at our pictures from the start.
I find you in my dreams,
In my silent screams.
I follow your hair as it cascades down,
Hiding my smile while you see me frown.
I think of the minutes we once spent—
If only you knew how much they meant.

I saw your eyes when they weren't looking at
me.
I saw someone else in the place I longed to be.
I wish I could fall out of love with you each
day,
But here I am, watching you from a mile
away.

Flashes

It feels like something's missing,
All the time—a part of my smile,
A part of my laugh.
Losing you, I don't feel enough.

Your memories find me
In empty spaces,
As my heart breathes in brisk paces.
I see your flashes as my heart lashes
Out and cries—I lost all I ever wanted.

And I wasn't capable of holding you close.
My tries were in vain, as I cried in pain,
Clutching the pillows close.
I mourn to sleep, missing you—

It feels like I'm missing a part of me.
As if I can't breathe without it,
As if I barely live without a life,
As I only survive,
One day at a time.

***

*What falls apart may not be broken; it may simply be
waiting to be found again.*

***

Frosted Fragments

Lost, and yet I waited for the night,
For unsaid words and thoughtless thoughts to
ignite.
A cold wind blew, and nothing was in sight,
Trapped in my world, entangled in my own
knots tight.

I shivered and cried through a dreary winter's
night,
Reasons unknown, in denial's silent plight.

Seeking warmth, I yearned for light,
Yet shadows lingered, eclipsing my fight.

I wasn't like this, not so long ago,
Once warm, loving, and full of life's glow.
Then something shifted, and things turned sore,
Succumbing to darkness in a moment of
uproar.

I shut it all down, turning off the dial,
Standing heartless and numb, cloaked in denial.
All that remained was a hollowed calm,
With the waning moon, so waned my charm.

Frozen like morning dew on a flower's bow,
Falling, melting, vanishing—hour by hour.
Alone amidst snowflakes, a life turned frail,
An echo of warmth, now a frosted trail.

***

*In every fragment of memory, there is a piece of love
that lingers.*

***

Worn by Your Love

I dive deep into your waters, clueless how to
swim,
I listen to your chatter, sleepless through the
nights.
I stood by you as you chose your lovers,
broken to the brim,
Scorned myself to sleep after every one of our
fights.

I was there for your joys, and shared in your
sorrows,
I've been through thick and thin, enduring
every one of your banters.

I was never too busy for you, even when time
was borrowed,
I knew ours was not meant to be a story, yet I
wrote our chapters.

I still lived up to my promises and stood by
you,
Through storms, numb nights, and everything
that matters.
I stood there as it ripped my soul, yet I
smiled, hoping you'd smile too,
I was used to your pain; I was insane to have
you by my side, spending myself with every
mile.

***

*Some loves are lost in silence, others in the words we
never dared to say.*

***

Half Hearted Love

She wasn't planned, the one I refer to here—
A tangled friendship, where love appeared.
I wasn't prepared to accept what was there;
Falling for a friend felt like an unfortunate
affair.

Caught in the turmoil, I knew what we
couldn't be.
Still, I tried to express my indelible love for
her—
Not through words, for friends cannot
confess.
I just stayed by her side,
Stretched thin, just to see her smile.

So you ask me, why do I call it half-hearted?
Because I cannot make her feel what I felt.
I knew that, yet I tried to get her off my
mind.
I was her go-to pal, and she was mine.

How could I love her and break this pledge?
It's hard to be by her side and feel this way.
We spent hours together, yet I still couldn't
say.
I planned to leave her and move far away,
Hoping my heart could beat for someone
else—
Someone who could reciprocate the words I
never said.

In and Out of Love

For I have not known why I fell for you, over
and over again.
And every time I did, I forced myself to fall
out of it—yet again.
You'll always be an entanglement I never
meant to happen,
And when it did, I couldn't stop thinking
how the idea of us was insane.

I did my best to push you out, depriving you
of my half-hearted affection—
Better than leaving you with this broken
mess,
This version of me who was unsure about you
from the start.
Just someone who used you to balance his
emotions,

A selfish need for attention hiding within his
heart.
But it feels so different today. It's your love I
crave,
The only thing that could balance this chaos
within me.
Even amidst the ripples of busy sounds,

I can constantly hear my heart whisper:
"Say it out loud—I miss you.
I fucked things up, the delicate dynamics of
what we used to be.
Hoping for just a little more,
I fell for you a little harder than I ever
thought I could be.

A Foolish Heart

Have you known heartbreak—
Walking through a lost abyss of endless steps,
With a feeling that leaves your heart sore to
beat?

Have you known heartbreak—
Yearning for sleep as silent tears flow,
While yesterday's hours were so easy to
repeat?
For I have known heartbreak,
Standing between nothingness and still.
Broken hearts and shattered memories—
A hollow remains, with nothing to fill.

For I have known heartbreak,
Reminiscing my efforts for you:
A void that lingers without your voice;
a smile that yearns for your laugh.

An apartment lying empty without your
presence,
A bed that feels lifeless without your essence,
A heart that stopped as you walked away.
And little have I done to ask you to stay.

Unspoken

I'm scared—scared of the silence you'd leave
behind,
Scared of the weight that would fall on my
spine.
Scared of being the one who must now stand
tall,
When all I want is to lean on you still.

I'm scared of a world without your voice,
Of carrying your legacy, unsure of my choice.
Scared that I'll fail to honor your name,
That I'll crumble beneath the weight of this
flame.

I'm scared of being a child without a father,
A wandering soul with no anchor to gather.
Scared there'll be no one to answer my pleas,
No one to guide me through life's stormy seas.

Scared that I'll lose the light in my eyes,
That I'll be left broken under hollow skies.
Scared of the ache in mom's quiet tears,
Of shielding my sister from unbearable fears.

Scared of the day I can't call you "Dad,"
Scared of advice that I'll never have had.
Scared of a life where you're just a name,
A memory carved at the edges of pain.

I'd be lost without you, a soul untethered,
Forever aching for moments we weathered.
And the deepest fear that will always stay—
That I couldn't do enough to make you stay.

Section 3: Whispers

"In silence there is eloquence. Stop weaving and watch how the pattern improves."

—Jalaluddin Rumi

Whispers are the truths we encounter in stillness, in the quiet moments between breaths. These poems reflect the echoes of solitude and the questions we carry within.

A Thought Trail

A web of thoughts clutters the corners of our
mind,
A string of unsettling thoughts,
interconnected, and tied.
We unscramble knots to count the odds in
our favor,
Ambitious goals coupled with insomniac
endeavors.

Our chariot moved wearily through the snow,
We kept pushing it forward, even if it was
slow.

The road was covered with a mist so dark,
We stood clueless, unsure if it was truly
darkness that lurked.

Unknown paths to unknown places,
Unsettling thoughts and unseen faces.
Yet,forward was the only way we marched,
Chasing dreams and goals that we had
marked.

Echoes of the Downpour

Thoughts rise to form thought clouds—
Clouds made up of feelings and emotions.
Clouds that are light with joy and laden with
sorrow.
A few clouds form from memories that never
get clouded.

They move as time passes,
Sometimes coagulating to form darker ones—
Ones so heavy they weigh down your heart.
Thoughts rise to form thought clouds—
Some are white and some are dark.

At times, there's lightning,
Striking at points that are dear,
Sending a shiver down my spine as the cold
settles in.
Thunderous roars,
Torments of those dark ones clashing
together.

The darkness spreads,
Covering the skies.
Drops tickle down my cheeks
And the downpour starts—
Some drip into my coffee as I sit there still.
That day it rained on both sides of the
window grill.

A Perplexed Traveller

A perplexed traveler rests beneath the
incandescent moonlight,
Scrounging his thoughts while his eyes sketch a
silent sight.

He gazes at the sky, where oblivion and distress
dance in fusion,
Turning the pages of his diary, contemplating a
notion.
His attempts were futile, as answers weren't
concealed in his past,
Unable to blend into his portrait, he
impersonates and mimes.

He looks at the moon, as the breeze touches his
tunic,
Penning his plights as a sonnet—melodic in its
music.

He was cheated, betrayed by the way he was
greeted,
What he followed was not what he needed.
Bewildered by his state of affairs, he smiles to
himself in hysteria—
Soon, he realised that dozing under the lonely
sky wasn't an eligibility criteria.

The weary traveler picks himself up and sets
sail,
Wandering aimlessly , trying to forget that he
might fail.

Downfall

I fall today into the deepest hollows of my
disintegrating dream.
"You failed yourself" —that's the only
sentence my heart can scream.
Succumbing to the darkest corners, I find a
place to weep,
Consoling the pain of a scar that ripped me
inordinately deep.

The heartache doesn't go away; it cripples my
thoughts instead.
I seek a chance to re-sketch fate, connecting
the dots left unsaid.

I tried, I did, I raised every bid—then why,
the world asks, did you?
They mock me as worthless, insolvent for
wasting pennies, maybe a few.

Little did they know those so-called
extravaganzas weren't for pleasure;
I spent it to cast away from expectations,
searching for closure.
No, I don't regret any time they say I wasted,
Because God didn't always provide me with
what I needed.
What I endured—how could I ever truly
construe?

I did what I had to and never took life to be
blue.
Then why, I ask myself, why? Is this the score
I've deserved?

Dear destiny, you keep puzzling me; please stop tarnishing my path,
I speak it out to you; you can hear, but not comprehend.
The agony leaps when I compare—why can't I just descend?

Intrinsic

My perturbed senses, my unwavering
plights—
I live today to lift myself, as I too deserve my
nights.
I free myself from unsettling ties, the strings
that pull me down.
I free my heart, my scars, my soul, as I claim
my own crown.

I am my king, and it's my duty—
To protect myself from internal torments and
wars.
I am my creator; I need no suitors—
I shine under my own stars.

It's my word, my welfare, and my well-being
that matters.
Broken shackles, broken chains—I break
everything that shatters.
I move on, step by step, toward the place I
long to be.
I live for my dreams, my happiness—
There's so much more in life for me to see.

Black

The shadows of fallen dreams that follow,
Prominent even in corners that are hollow.
The plethora of plights subtly masked in your
vain crusades,
The nothingness that lies beneath all
masquerades.
The colour of the blood that has bled and
dried,
Shed from the slumped attempts that you
tried.

The temptations that find you in your lonely
passages,
The hole in that boat you row on your
voyages.
The heresy of that rebellion you led amidst
your odds,
The prominence of strength that clouds your
flaws.
The grit that you carry to push amidst the
dark—
You embraced that colour and wore it to be
stark.

Fading Innocence

The simplicity lost in the haze of our growing senses,
When we dreamt freely, without the bounds of reality's fences.
Our crayons portrayed psychedelic shades of our emotions,
When we weren't tamed by the clock's circular motions.

Our curiosity peeked from behind the veils of innocence,
When we weren't forced to seek hope from patience.

We were little—cute, happy, and smitten. Gone are those days, when we were just children.

Slippers in the Snow

So how do you be kind to yourself, I ask,
When you row a boat endlessly without a
destination,
As your heart is swayed by every passing
infatuation—
Can you have it all?
The answer's no. Then why chase it amidst frost
and snow?
Have you forgotten to wear your slippers?
How can you run if your feet are numb with
frost?
Cursing your own missteps will not bring
peace—
You cannot conquer every sea.

Why push yourself
Deeper into the abyss
Why repeat to yourself
Harsh words born from those you love?
Isn't it kindness your soul truly starves?
Treading through storms with a broken heart is
harder—
Could a smile help you make it further?
Do you not deserve to unlearn this oath,
To release your mind from these self-imposed
ties?
I am not asking you to sugar-coat with rosy
lies—
Only to soften the edge of your inner cries.
Then why refuse that gentle grace?
Why shed a tear at every mile?
Can you carry on with a kinder heart?
Be gentle with yourself, even if you must
restart.

***

The spaces we leave behind stay within us,
even as the world moves us forward

***

Another Cog in the Wheel

"After chasing glory and excellence all my life,
I find myself tangled in reality's quiet strife.
Does any of this truly matter?
What is it you ask of me?

Stuck, like another nameless cog in the
wheel's churn,
I spin through days as I crash and burn.
A boy molded by the weight of societal
expectations,
Now a man lost in his monthly calculations.

I've forgotten how it feels to dream,
Content with my thirty paid leaves a year—.
I cherish a paycheck as if it were gold,
Chasing titles as the fire in my heart grows
cold.

My guitar lurks alone in the corner, growing
old;
Spreadsheets take all my time—my passions
sold.
I praise the bars of this comfortable cage,
Even as it robs me of my loved ones' stage.
No time to nurse my health or ease my
mind—
I labor to swell another's bottom line.

The work I trade my soul for—
What is it really for?
A mere decimal in the economy's tide,
A number for a boss's pride,

Why should I bear the brunt of it all—
When I am your scapegoat for when things
fall.

Why does my competence change with your
mood?
Sometimes saying "you could have done
more" is rude.
You shrink my worth with careless ease—
Sleeping with your work is an inflicted
disease.
Exceeding your expectations shouldn't be my
goal
Wasn't freedom the birthright of my soul?

A puppet tugged by strings thinning with
each year,
no matter what I mint, it's never enough.
I impersonate a robot amidst these
skyscrapers-
My dreams disintegrate with each ill
appraisal's dose.
I once claimed I was clever, yet here I remain,
Spinning in capitalism's ceaseless grind
Spending pennies a few is my precious win.
Was earning less, my biggest sin?

I've made peace with being another cog,
Forgotten the fire that once broke the fog.
But even as I turn, I wonder still—
Is this my life, or someone else's will?

***

In the quietest moments,
we hear the call of the places we belong.
***

Home

What do you call your home, my friend?
Is it the weight of dreams you must defend,
The parental hopes, both loud and unspoken,
Or love so "unconditional," but often broken?

Is it the bed where restless nights reside,
Or the meals your mother makes with pride?
The familiar scent of walls you've known,
Or a space that's yours, yet not your own?

What do you call home in this race,
Is it a rented room, a fleeting place?

The shades of curtains, the rules you bend,
Or the hollow silence at each day's end?
Is it the couch where your weekends blur,
Or the freedom to choose who you were?

Does it hold your fears, your hidden scars,
Or cradle your dreams beneath the stars?
Is it where you unwind, at your own pace,
A fleeting refuge, a comforting space?

Empty halls and ever-changing keys,
Skyscrapers swaying in the city breeze,
What is it, truly, that you call home—
A place, a feeling, or where you roam?

For me, my home is not a place,
Not walls, nor rooms, nor empty space.
It's her, the one I return to each night,
Her love, my harbor, my guiding light.

Her laughter fills the void with song,
With her, my spirit feels ever strong.
So ask me again what I call my own—
For me, my home is her alone.

End Note

Thank you for joining me on this journey through love, loss, and quiet introspection. Each poem in Fossils of a Fleeting Life was written during a fleeting moment I wanted to hold onto, and knowing these words have found their way to you makes the effort worthwhile.

If this book resonated with you, I would love to hear your thoughts. Whether it's a review on platforms like Amazon or Goodreads, or simply sharing your favorite poem on social media, your reflections help bring these pages to life in ways I could achieve alone.

This book is a small reminder that life, in all its impermanence, still holds beauty worth cherishing. Thank you for allowing these fragments of my story to become part of yours.

With gratitude,
Aninda Halder

www.ingramcontent.com/pod-product-compliance
Lightning Source LLC
LaVergne TN
LVHW050919200726
843508LV00011B/2228

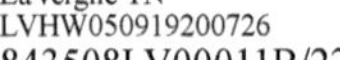